Rochelle Owens *Futz*

Who Do You Want, Peire Vidal?

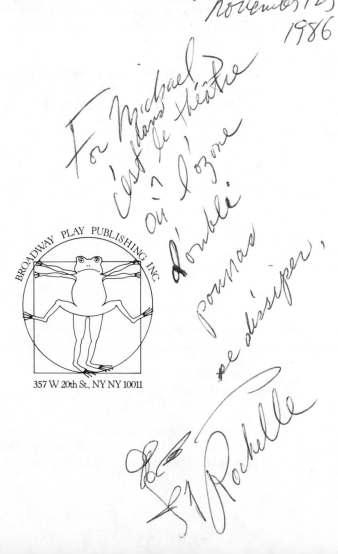

November 12, 1986

*For Michael,
c'est dans le théâtre
où l'ozone
d'oubli
pouvons
se dissiper,
Rochelle*

BROADWAY PLAY PUBLISHING INC.

357 W 20th St., NY NY 10011

First printing: July 1986
ISBN: 0-88145-040-5

Design by Marie Donovan
Set in Aster by L&F Technical Composition, Lakeland, FL
Printed and bound by Cushing-Malloy, Inc., Ann Arbor, MI

For my friends

Ann and Don Farber
Elaine and Harmon Shragge
Barbara and Howard Wise

ABOUT THE AUTHOR

Rochelle Owens is a poet as well as a playwright of many innovative and controversial plays. A pioneer in the experimental off-Broadway theatre movement, she has received several *Village Voice* Obie Awards and Honors from the *New York Drama Critics Circle*. Her plays have been presented at festivals in Edinburgh, Avignon, and Berlin. Since its first publication in 1961, *Futz* has become a classic of the American avant-garde theatre and an international success; the play was made into a film which has itself attained the status of a cult following. Her plays and poetry have been translated into numerous languages. She has published twelve books of poetry and two collections of plays, *Futz and What Came After*, and *The Karl Marx Play and Others*. She has edited *Spontaneous Combustion*: Eight New American Plays. Several of her plays are included in *The Best Short Plays* anthologies. A member of the Dramatists Guild, A.S.C.A.P. and a recipient of Guggenheim, CAPS, Yale School of Drama, N.E.A. and Rockefeller grants, she was invited to contribute an essay on her life and work to *Contemporary Authors*, Autobiography Series (Gale Research). After living many years in New York City, she currently resides in Norman, Oklahoma. She has taught at the University of California and the University of Oklahoma where she was the host of an important interview series program called *The Writer's Mind*. She has given many readings, performance events, and workshops in the United States and abroad, including the American College in Paris and Kings College in London. Her latest play is entitled *Three Front*. Her current projects include a video-theatre piece and the dramatization of sections of two long series poems entitled *How Much Paint Does The Painting Need* and *W.C. Fields In French Light*. The Mugar Library of Boston University, the library of the University of California at Davis, the library of the University of Oklahoma, and the Rodgers and Hammerstein Archives Library & Museum of the Performing Arts at The New York Public Library all house special collections of her manuscripts, tapes, papers, and memorabilia.

INTRODUCTION

In 1958, I wrote my first play, *Futz*. I had been working as a clerk in the accounting department at Sotheby-Parke Bernet Galleries. Among the customers were Greta Garbo, Ali Khan, and Katherine Hepburn. The early drafts of the play were typed on lot statements and sheets torn from the daily calendar. Between sales, during the slow periods, I would write, secretly, my play. In the evenings at home I'd eagerly work for hours, transcending everyday reality with the surprises, discovery, and fulfillment of artistic creativity. Because of the success of *The String Game* and *Istanboul*, later plays of mine (*Istanboul* had garnered a *Village Voice* Obie), I acquired an agent, and in 1965 *Futz* was produced as a work-in-progress under the auspices of the Office of Advanced Drama Research at the Tyrone Guthrie Theatre and the University of Minnesota. Two years earlier, the Living Theatre had planned it for production. The project was cancelled because of tax difficulties the company encountered.

In 1967 *Futz* was produced by Ellen Stewart at the LaMama Experimental Theatre Club. It won the three top *Village Voice* Obie Awards: Best Play, Best Direction, and Best Actor. It became an international success and the hit of the famed Edinburgh festival. During its long New York run, a performance was cancelled when Robert Kennedy was assassinated.

The *London Observer* described *Futz* as "The most exciting American theatre since Miller, Williams, and Albee," and Edith Oliver of *The New Yorker* called it "a witty, harsh, farcical, and touching dramatic poem about the love—romantic, domestic and sexual—of a farmer for his pig, a love that demoralizes his amoral, brainless neighbors, driving them, variously, to lunacy, incest and murder." In 1969 the film version premiered in New York City. The film was faithful to the text of the play and I wrote some additional dialogue; as always, Tom O'Horgan, the director, and I worked well together.

In 1978 I met Richard Caron, the French director who had premiered *Futz* at the Festival d'Avignon. During that time I had been impressed with his directorial concept and was interested in his translating a new play of mine into French and staging it at his cafe-theatre in Paris. During my visit I saw a rehearsal of my play *Who do You Want, Peire Vidal?* and admired the actors and the translation very much. In 1982 the play premiered in New York City at the Theatre for the New City. Anarchistic in form and tone, its dramatic scenes interspersed with music, monologues, and pantomime, the play represents two characters in a continuing state of colliding frames of mind. The *Village Voice* described *Who Do You Want, Peire Vidal?* as "explosions of parody, eroticism, and violence, eruptions of the id and the intellect . . . extremely engaging, surprising . . . marvelous extravagance of language."

Recently, after having viewed the film *Futz* based on my play, and after re-reading the text of the play, I became strongly aware of the proto-feminist nature of the work. During the panel discussion held after a screening at the University of Oklahoma in April 1984, some of the audience remarked that the cruel truths of the women's lives were fixed in an extraordinary way; feminist criticism would add a new dimension to the complexities of my dramatic literature.

I am interested in what has previously been ignored or neglected in my plays except by one writer, Joan Goulianos, in the *Village Voice* of February 4, 1971, in an interview called "Getting Rid of Thou Shalt Not." Even the more efficient and astute critics have been perhaps more narrow or rigid than they ever suspected when it came to the revelation of a world of outraged and angry female protagonists who fill the landscapes of some of my plays. A feminist perspective would enrich the aesthetic and multifaceted interpretations that have been given to my work.

Still, the points of origin lie deep within one, and the finished work outlasts without denying the array of perspectives it evokes.

"I have an image of you in my mind, poking like a finger under my eyelids. You're standing next to a vase filled with wildflowers. My ego is growing claws that are ready to tear off a piece of whatever I can get them into. There is no pattern to my life that you can understand. I have a hunch, you'll find yourself basking in the sun with me one of these days—but the odds are against it. You'll most likely die in a mental institution at a ripe old age. What do you think of when you look at the old photographs of us together? Do you feel as though you walked away from a head-on collision? I talk to you—you refuse to understand. I loved the way you moved your body — and not once have I pitched woo with anybody but you, dear." Rochelle Owens' *Chucky's Hunch.*

The above quote is one of my official manifestos, a theory of my approach to writing. It is my savage muse talking to me.

ROCHELLE OWENS

Futz

Futz was first presented for one performance on October 10, 1965, at the Tyrone Guthrie Workshop at the Minnesota Theatre Company. It was then presented by the LaMama Troupe on March 1, 1967, at The LaMama Theatre in New York City, with the following cast:

(In order of appearance)

Narrator .... Beverly Atkinson
Cyrus Futz .... John Bakos
Majorie Satz .... Beth Porter
Oscar Loop .... Seth Allen
Bill Marjoram .... Michael Warren Powell
Keeper .... Peter Craig
Ann Fox .... Mari-Claire Charba
Sheriff Tom Sluck .... Peter Craig
Father Satz .... Rob Thirkield
Mother Satz .... Mari-Claire Charba
Brother Ned Satz .... Victor LiPari
Mrs. Loop .... Marilyn Roberts
Warden .... Peter Craig
Sugford .... Michael Warren Powell
Buford .... Peter Craig

The Music and Direction were by Tom O'Horgan. The set was designed by Saito. Laura Rambaldi designed the Lighting, and Howard Vishinsky provided Technical Assistance.

Author's Notes

The various settings of the play may be simply suggested with a minimum of props. The techniques of film, especially montage, quick-cutting, lighting, and musical backup, should be utilized. It is important that the director keep in mind the dynamics of rhythm, imagery, and tonal "meanings" within the language. The actor has worlds within worlds to play. The elements of humor ought to be found so that the darker aspects emerge with stronger impact.

Except for the characters Cyrus Futz, Majorie Satz, and Oscar Loop, the actors can double in the other roles.

Now concerning the things whereof ye wrote unto me: It is good for a man not to touch a woman.

I Corinthians 7:1

Scene One

NARRATOR: Let's give it a stange passion to a story, some handyman handy in the barns with animals—"someone to watch over him"—somethings, the udders of the moo-moo especially. No stupid pretty girl to rely on him, like a homemade stunt between his feet, to knock up his knees —bad onions—spoiling him eternally. Small fetid room, obvious barn-like, but still a small room with lots of oily automobile rags and other signs of the terrible city existence, brewed still more stinky with the worst the country has to offer—dead grassy worms; horses' shit; small portions of a moldy outhouse; summer brooms; women's drawers; rubber suits for working in the water; etc. Anything you can think up naturally. Cy Futz, a Scandinavian sort of big fellow, wearing new dungarees, bell bottom, they could be overalls, comes in filled with a sexual dream; it does not bear in the least to anything real in terms of yours or Cy's world. It's pure sickness, but in its pureness it's a truth. Sitting down on a wet broken step, he says:

CY: O the cow's tits are bigger and I know it's wrong, but young uns never know the difference between an animal's or a woman's hip bones, so soft like my socks, fresh washed like new kid's hoofs. O I could sing. OOOOOoooOOOOOooooo OOOO LooLoooooooooLOOOOOOO Looy LOOY LOY LORD LORD I LOVE YOU GOD. And I have no hate for anybody, but wanting to love the animals the way I do. *They*, mean folks hate my face. I turn around the corners and make fun on their asses, no tickle does theirs feel like my own good one as I sing tears in the sow's belly. With their fried eggs for wives, they know no song.

NARRATOR: Again he sings his ooo's and looooo's intermingled with a belch and a mock fart and ending with three very loud "Lords." All the time he's buttering his wrists with his red hands, making bird and other noises, he is very excited and seems absolutely certain to explode all his love or whatever over the world which is the room where he is in now. Now she comes in, Miss Majorie Satz, about twenty-seven years old, tall with a square worldly, insulted once maybe, body. Her coarse red hair is combed up in a sophisticated way which is sweetly silly in retrospect to her food-stained gingham, typical farm girl get-up.

MAJORIE: Hello Bastady man. Yus big man-bloke, I missed you at the greengrocer, yus said that you would come, yus said so, and I painted my big toe too for yu. (*Giggling*) Yu man-bloke, old Swede man.

NARRATOR: Cyrus is looking at her and is vexed at her, probably Cy was always squinnied by her, probably because she obviously is a woman in the very dreamy sensual way which he only wants his animals to be. Gentle sick man he is. He hoots at her.

CY: Hallas Majy Ya French dancer! You woman of ten beds and manure heaps, yus stinking human woman with only cat-mouths for tits and a baby-paw for your arse. I did not want to see you, you told me a foul story the last time that I saw you. Not again mind you do I want that shit! Always you are pretending to be my friend and better yet a hole for me to dive in, but I'd rather sink my pick in turd, cleaner my Lord more than you Maj! Nahhh! I don't want no sow with two feet but with four! Them repeats true things with their grunts not like you human-daughter.

NARRATOR: Majorie moves backwards and starts to hum the French anthem.

MAJORIE: I'll pick up my skirt right now if yu want. I'll get on my heels and elbows, old farmer, yus not so old yu know only forty, there are whut's younger men than yu who'd like to take me to a movie, strongir and slimmir than yu, so why make me hurt your chest—an' don't I buy you fodder for your sick love, Amanda the sow, so she could be a better one for yu? Even I know, who likes yu, how bud it is to sleep with a pig! Unnatural, like in the

Bible, it's piggish—that's where the word comes from yus know piggish—from a pig yugh yugh sooo evil. Yu smell so baad it is no joke—

CY: Go forget about it and your cheeks won't be nervous—put your nose out of my business, disgusting girl. I like Amanda because she's good. Pig or not. And I don't stink that's your lie—any much more than you or the boys that take you in the fields.

MAJORIE: (*Hatefully*) That's your awn dirtty story 'nd it maks me nasty towards yu—I can't feel bad for your dread and doom—yu sleep with the unimals bitter bitter unholy unholy.

NARRATOR: Cy pushes her from behind, then stoops and picks up a dirty broom, begins to sweep her flanks with a mock lust, also singing a very low song in a Celtic tune. She covers her ears and shreiks.

MAJORIE: Yeeeiiiiey Oyu Big man-bloke!

NARRATOR: He snaps her rope belt with his left hand and slaps her face (not hard)* with the right. He pushes her ahead of him and they both go behind the half-rotten wall which was once an old outhouse.

(*Animal grunts sound and the lights are dimmed.*)

SCENE TWO

NARRATOR: Look at the old rotten wall—behind it, here are Cyrus and Maj and yugch! a sow. Amanda! The animal that's sure to steal forever Cy's heart (never to marry) yus, her, Maj, sweet flower, woman with a wholesome grin, and no hair on the chin, sallow woman with a cantaloupe seed in her belly and toes that are canary yellow. Ooopph.

(NARRATOR *pushes his hands in a cup form and feeds the sounds of grunts and human voice to the audience.*)

Stage directions are either performed by the actors or verbalized by the narrator. This is left to the decision of the director.

MAJORIE: Pechhh *so* indecent, I'd live in shame if the village ever knew what I'd done.

CY: Fahhh my woman the people need never know what you done, anyways they would want the full freedom to be able to do what you done. Girl, peachy sweet currant stop being afraid, even the sow won't tell!

NARRATOR: Maj tears, she's sore afraid.

MAJORIE: Yu make it wus tan it is mentionin' the pig—she does not know anyting about it, and she did not feel soft like you said but like an old razor on my feet. O o o so indecent I am, and now the filty dreams 'ill come. O Gods help meee that we shoulda both laid with a sow.

NARRATOR: Maj carries about awhile with hands scratching out her Lord from the sky, pushing him into her soul, trying to wring his sweat from the skinny body, trying hard hard to have his water wash the dinny sin from her wretched body. Lust for animals is like a run in spring rain. (Sniggle) Lewd lewd, foosh foosh, and she calls on all the idols and the true god to make the slop go away.

CY: Now fish stop, stop fish, nobody knows and the pig won't tell.

MAJORIE: Stop stop stop! Yus mean rat, your modern sin has killed me!

CY: Isn't no modern sin, old as your Bible, lay down with a calf somebody did and did get no punishment from God, like your village will give you. Cluck, if you don't stop your sirens blowing, shit your mouth up Majorie, you're makin' me sound funny in my own ears and I have faith for my love of the animals with hoofs and corncob appitite, can't you really see—it is no wrong. They laugh more real than the mayor and your mother. Brooey to the devil for the bad conscience you feel, say phat phat to it. It don't pay.

MAJORIE: Your diggnitty is like sloppy ole shoes, but good luck to me, soon as I get away from evil—never again. Os Os never agin piggiying myself like that.

NARRATOR: She gets up from the bed of wet paper and rags, smoothing her clothes and wrapping her hair in her fists. Cy watches her with pickles in his eyes. He spys the pig and on the knees and hands jerks towards her, sticking his fingers out like stone worms, his tongue lolls like mice in his mouth, he sticks his leg out, banging his shoe on the pig's ass (not cruelly though) just enough to make the animal turn and be conscious of him, for in that white-flesh no-blood brain she remembers pleasure. And she backs towards him you know and he grabs her body. Maj is watching with bloody senses, then tears out shrieking.

SCENE THREE

NARRATOR: In an old-fashioned prison cell with the traditional water pot, hammock, etc., two men are talking (O everything is the same with these two as with a hundred other yolts). The jailbird, Oscar Loop, is skinny and wears the prison suit like he was a fallen priest, the other man is Bill Marjoram, squat, strong, sweaty and typical in work clothes, fat shoes, etc., how can well I go describing on?

LOOP: O breadfast is not much, I mean breakfast is not much, two pieces of bread, glass of water and a sausage, not real you know, something to think about anyway, sometimes I think like a motherless child, I mean take the tiny spices out of the sausage and grow them like small insects, I mean if they get watered and sun on them they might get life and then they'd be like insects.

BILL: Shut up, Loop! Stupid, talking 'bout insex and maybe hanging tomorra! Your riddles too! Make me sick.

LOOP: Listen, they would be spice insects, so you could eat them—they would even be medicinal, cure a palsy helpfully, jerk a dead newborn back to life. O I hope it would do all those things.

BILL: Shut up, Loop! I said. Stupid. Don't you know you gonna die?

Loop: I mean a dead newborn could have been Mozart—I care in a great many ways for life, that's why the good sausage seed-spice might work (*Whispers*) without the evil eye, I bet Siva would help me, Siva is beautiful with her lovely hands, she's picked the mosquitoes out of my head. I've read greatly about her.

Bill: You keep blabbing on 'nd on 'bout things that don't stop you from dying!

Loop: How do you know? What makes you be so sure? Anything cun help a man maybe, a rock hit a devil in the Bibledays and a devil sucked out the blood of the thrower of that rock in hell. Somebody made that devil draw out all the blood in the man. Hmmmmmmmmmmmmmmmmm I'll have to write that on the sausage. Mustn't forgit all the marvelous thoughts I git lately.

Bill: Mavilous thoughts my foot! Swear you're gonna hang on Monday. Man, think, Loop! Think! Whut did you do?

Loop: Whut did I do? Flah! A woman saw me, she bought me a mitten, tole me to put it on, said that the feeling would come through better. She looked like Mary in a story, but not the Lord's mother you know. No she looked like the whore. But then like him I changed her.

Bill: Whut do you mean, changed her! Speak it up truthfully. You killed her!

Loop: I made her fall asleep on the ground. Put a bad blueberry in her mouth, Satan was a grub, and when he got inside of her he ate her innards out but that was God's wish.

Narrator: Loop is smiling like a good king.

Bill: How did she die? And if it's too bad a story, you bitter not tell it in your crazy way. Tell me how you killed the girl, nobody dies with fruitbugs, tell it sound and real.

Narrator: Now there are keys and chains sounds, the prison keeper comes in and Loop, eyes frightened, begins to stretch. He is afraid that he has been heard.

(*Everybody cringes.*)

LOOP: I mean to say that what I tole Bill wasn't all so. (*Points to the keeper and ropes his arm toward himself.*) You come here, guard, O I'm gonna tell you how I killed the girl, but in the beginning. Hoos! In the beginning was purity, and cleanliness was a big garter belt.

NARRATOR: The keeper is sniffing in his giggles, feeling his bone, trying to see garter belts.

KEEPER: Tell us what happened and maybe you can get a reprieve, hhah ha ha ha hiss—Did you put the garter belt 'round her small throat?

LOOP: I met Ann Fox in the greengrocer's. I saw her skirt swing frisky, and I knew that her father was a good farmer and Baptist. I knew that everybody in the village liked that family. And no young fella would treat her disrespectfully. I could not just get married to a girl, without her being like Ann, I knew that I wouldn't get married and be normal—so I asked her out, and she went with me, she said she liked the smell of leather. You know I have a good leather belt and jacket that a handcrafts woman sent me. Well Ann liked that jacket, she said she'd take it from me when I was asleep. Sometimes I think she meant it too. Her father was a rich man, he could buy her all the leather clothes she wanted but she'd say she wanted my jacket too. Well I'd get mad thinking about it, though I knew too that she was playing. But I took her one night near the field where Cy Futz's barn is and we horseplayed a little bit, nothing but some hunky-punk.

SCENE FOUR

NARRATOR: A small dark field, nighttime, a blanket on the grass, a leather jacket spread perfectly out. Oscar Loop and Ann Fox are sitting opposite each other cross-legged.

LOOP: Little good cat, ooph you knock my eyes out of my head, you're so pretty.

NARRATOR: He sticks out his forefinger and strokes her nose.

ANN: Buford Skark says I'm pretty too, too bad to mention another fella? You both think the same, that I'm pretty.

NARRATOR: Loop hops on his knees hooping himself toward her (if it's possible lights should shine green on top of his hair).

LOOP: Little rat stop thinkin' of other men! Dogs 'ill crawl up your back if you do.

NARRATOR: He puts his hands on her hips and she falls at him laughing. They both move at each other like beach balls. Her foot catches in the jacket and he pushes at her ankle with two hands. She meanly slams her shoe into the precious leather.

LOOP: Crazy rich girl cut that out!

ANN: Hang it!

LOOP: Whut d'yu mean hang it! Have respect for a man's garment. I wear that on Sunday!

ANN: On Sunday the people laugh at you too just like on Monday. Ooooobles you're serious, so, so serious. Why'nt you kiss me? I'm a girl.

LOOP: I I I will kiss you—I would like to learn to dance, so that I can go with you to fancy places.

NARRATOR: She moves her hip closer to his and takes his hand laying it on her stomach. He grabs her mightily and they kiss.

ANN: I hear something, is it my head? There are crazy bees inside of it, you kiss crazy. (*Sounds, like those of an animal in heat, are heard.*) Listen—I hear grunts! And I think someone cussing. Don't it sound strange?

LOOP: Yus, I hear them too. Don't know why somebody should beat their animals. Terrible to do that—I would never do that.

NARRATOR: Loop and Ann move very close to where the noises come from. Futz's barn. The barn is not seen though. The noise is a human and animal one. And both people are dumbstruck at what in all heaven's holy name is happening. Something equally weird is happening to Loop; he looks insane. He pushes himself at Ann and starts to pummel her, his voice is croaky.

LOOP: Gonna rid the place of evil, gonna make you sleep a long time till your soul becomes clean.

ANN: (*She screams*) Stop it stop it! Let me be.

NARRATOR: She tries to get away but he drags her around in a small circle.

LOOP: Gonna bury you in that evil dress, stink will in a hundred years be covered up by the sweet grass, hell isn't as bad as a whoring girl. May your father and mother not mourn you too long.

NARRATOR: Ann cries in soulful anguish. Loop drags her off. He comes back in terribly bloody clothes and sits cross-legged in the moony night. The animal sounds are louder but he shows no life, just sits with his arms folded and the hands covering his eyes. Then he slowly takes off his shoes and with a monkey's grace raises his feet to his nose and whiffs deeply.

SCENE FIVE

NARRATOR: Cy Futz's barn again just like in the beginning. Cy is sitting with his kneebones high like the two hemispheres. The pig Amanda is sleeping on her side.

CY: Flahfy Amanda ya faymale! Four ugly legs yu got, Zeus wot hams. Lucky luck that I'm in love with you otherwise you'd be hanging in my pantry. Heeeehhhhehehehe when you're old you'll be sitting in my granny's rockin' chair readin' the Bible. Amanda you are of the world, known two kinds of male animals, pig and man! Sow I know you love me but I wonder whether you'd rather be with your own kind? Piglets I can't give you you know though I am a healthy man.

NARRATOR: Cy licks his hands passionately and praises God for making him a husbandman. Silent is his worship but the world enters his barn now. Bill Marjoram and the Sheriff Tom Sluck, slowly they go up to him. Futz yawns one eye open.

MARJORAM: There's the creep!

SLUCK: Y'all be quiet now.

MARJORAM: Quiet in hell, the biggest sinner in the world is here. If we weren't fair he'd be dead now by our own hands.

CY: I'd break them off like they were rabbits' necks.

SLUCK: Nothing is really proven yet. There will be justice.

MARJORAM: Men can make men insane!

SLUCK: Nothing is really proven yet.

MARJORAM: He drove a fella wacky!

CY: Fitz on you both boys! I know no man well enough to make him nuts. Tell me who's crazy?

SLUCK: A man's in jail now for murdering a girl, he killed because he saw something very evil.

CY: Very sad thing. But there's lotsa evil here in the world.

MARJORAM: You're the satan here in our village!

CY: I'm not anybody's keeper. I'm never near anybody. Except when they come here to see me. I just work on my little plot of land raisin' vegetables for me and my pig. What sort of evil could I have done?

NARRATOR: Cy plays a tom-tom with his feet, and salutes the sun. This is done subtly, the men not being aware of the ritual. Lord these two are blind!

SLUCK: The man who murdered an innocent girl says he did it because he was under an influence, a spell he says, because he's a simple man. Now Mr. Futz I'm going to be blunt. People say here that you are an unnatural man.

CY: Am I?

SLUCK: Well, aren't you?

MARJORAM: Gods he bangs pigs!

CY: I never do. Why my mother didn't bring me up like that. I'm a Bible man.

SLUCK: If you're not serious you better become it. Very many people talk about your way.

CY: They're all wrong Mr. Sluck. An animal is something to care about, not to commiteth a sin with. Soos!

MARJORAM: See what he says! Soos!

SLUCK: Soos! Soos! What does it mean?

MARJORAM: It means he be guilty and pulling our feet.

CY: Why why I never would go with an animal! I'm a village man and the sun is good on me, why I say that fellow has a devil in his head.

(*He points at* MARJORAM.)

MARJORAM: Devils you bastard!

NARRATOR: He lunges at Cy and throws him down; he should not have done that though because Futz is quick and kicks his legs out cracking Marjoram's guts hard. The Sheriff fires his pistol a warning shot into the air. Both men relax like drugged sheep.

SLUCK: There will be a trial for the man who killed the girl and he'll probably hang! The day will be Monday!

CY: I do wish they, folks, wouldn't be mean toward each other.

MARJORAM: Mean! He talks about not bein' mean! Whut about Majorie Satz? She's wretched. She's become a bigger tart than she was. She's yapping always about what he did with her and the pig with him, at the same time too he was with her. Crazy evil! Heaven help us working people with Lucifer here in our village!

SLUCK: What are you laughing for? It ain't funny when a man's going to die.

CY: I'm not killing, I'm not a judge or lawyer, just a farmer who lives poorly mindin' his own business.

MARJORAM: Well my word! You live here in the town with us. Where's your duty and responsibility?

CY: In my hands. I use them only on my land and in my barn.

SLUCK: I'm gonna tell you that I hate you myself. It isn't right that I as a lawman feel that way. The Constitution says that there should be fairness. But you ruined women, animals and a man's going to die because of you. Futz, I'm gonna do something that my sweet guts don't want, I'm gonna lock you up in the prison because the people might come here, my choppers say yes to your head under their feet, taking good revenge. But I'm gonna lock you up. You'll be safe.

CY: Who'll feed my pig and water my vegetables?

SLUCK: That's not our thought to care about your land and animals. My duty's gonna be lockin' you up in a cell.

MARJORAM: I think he needs death, not just bein' locked up. Futz had done so much harm.

SLUCK: He'll be locked up.

NARRATOR: Futz hurls up his arms as though ready to receive lightning sticks from his friend god, crash them down on the heads of his judgers who want to see him minus, with no thing, no bliss.

CY: I'm a helpless man now, a partridge run after by turkeys!

MARJORAM: Bastud. Lecherous bastud. You'll get yours for spoilin' our lives.

SLUCK: I'll be easier when you pay up your debt to us. You've done a wrong, man.

NARRATOR: Futz in the middle walks out with the men, maybe sad jazz could be played now, not too much though.

SCENE SIX

NARRATOR: Majorie Satz, it's another day, in the field with two men, father and brother. The first is simple. The second is complex.

FATHER: I don't know what about anything but Futz should hang though.

BROTHER NED: Like Loop, Dad. And the corpses hosswhipped.

NARRATOR: Majorie is quiet with her arms hard against her body. She's listening like water.

FATHER: My dotter Majie is a good girl. Frisky like her reverent mother.

(*The old man slaps* MAJORIE'S *face.*)

MAJORIE: Git away from me ya old creep. Nothing was my fault!

BROTHER NED: Dad, cut it out! Nothin' is the girl's fault. She's just crazy.

FATHER: She is crazy! Should be put away!

MAJORIE: Can't be solved this way, nothing can, important thing is that I get revenged.

BROTHER NED: Nobody gonna revenge you! Nobody really cares that much.

FATHER: I care. Who's gonna marry this tramp if somehow we don't save her honor. Nobody'll git the bitch off my neck if Futz is allowed to get away with what he done.

She's gotta get married off or I'll have her around our shack forever.

NARRATOR: The old man is sick by this fact of life.

FATHER: She's just got to be made respectable.

BROTHER NED: Don't Bill Marjoram want to marry her? I get the idea he'd be willing to have the ole slot machine.

MAJORIE: Shet up, ya bastud. Don't call me names.

FATHER: Control that trap! It's a wonder you haven't been killed yet being whut you are. Majorie, you're a poisonous snake. And if I didn't have to live in this village I'd kill you myself. Your daddy or not—I hate you!

NARRATOR: Does Satz mean it? I don't know.

BROTHER NED: The both of you really get me! Spoiling with fight when we got to think of something. Something where we can get Futz. I mean he should be killed! Loop is gonna be killed and Futz should also.

NARRATOR: Brother does not have much feeling when he says this. Does he have a reason for Futz's death? Yes. His sister's honor? No. Well . . .

FATHER: I don't want a ruckus and yet there's gotta be something to happen.

MAJORIE: What he does with animals is dirty.

BROTHER NED: HAHAHaaaahshhhhushy yeah yeah.

FATHER: Craziest thing I ever heard of.

BROTHER NED: Maybe it's good?

MAJORIE: OOOOOOOOOOOOooooooooooohhhh I'm sick!

FATHER: Stop your yellin', tramp. You've muddied yaself with every bloke in the village.

MAJORIE: So I have. But it's with men.

FATHER: Quit up your braggin'. Slut!

BROTHER NED: She sure is.

(BROTHER NED *hunches over with jackal laughter.*)

SCENE SEVEN

NARRATOR: Oscar Loop is in his cell; his mother is there. She looks like Loop, smaller of course, and wearing old things. It's the day of her boy's death.

MRS. LOOP: Oscar, sweet good boy. I didn't do nothing but, but good for you I thought. I told you 'bout God when you were small and polished up your shoes for you when you went to school. I did my best for you, my son.

(*She weeps.*)

LOOP: Mama, I know you did, Mama, I know you did. But let's make some plans for the wonderful things that I have. (*Takes from his pocket tiny specks of something.*) Mama, these are holy bits of something good. They can cause miracles. Make people that are sick well. You know. They can even make a dead thing come alive again.

MRS. LOOP: Let me hold some in my hand, maybe it'll cure my arthritis. What are they, my son?

LOOP: I call them spice-seed insects, they're alive.

NARRATOR: Mother flings her arms to the north and south, letting the insects fly. She squelches a shriek letting something dawn on her. Her son's dream.

MRS. LOOP: O son, I'm sorry. But those wonderful seeds are potent, they cured my arthritis so quickly, my hands tingle.

LOOP: I knew it would work. I'm so happy. Take care of them I only have a handful. Mother use them wisely, don't give them to no pretty woman, only old people and dead things. It's a gift from Siva.

MRS. LOOP: Siva? Who is Siva?

LOOP: A holy thing with lots of arms. She couldn't die with her lots of arms, even if ten brutes tried to do her in. Siva lives and lives.

MRS. LOOP: Siva sounds like she's a good Christian woman. None around here like her. My son hates evil so he justly killed it. Oh son. Oh son, that you should be killed by the villagers is fair though you're my precious blood, it's right. And that you should have killed an evil girl, is right too. No! Nobody—no woman is good, all want one thing from a man, his lust stick!

LOOP: Mother mother mother (*He is weeping.*) mother mother mother why couldn't I find you? Why couldn't I ha' been my own father.

MRS. LOOP: Stop it my son (*She is slightly smiling.*), that is not a thing to say, but we two are godly and there shall be rest for us both. A son and his mother are godly.

LOOP: A son-and-his-mother-are-godly. Everything you say is beautiful. Mother, you are like the holy virgin.

MRS. LOOP: That is blasphemy, son. Never say that. Look! Look! Look at me, my boy, watch me. Don't talk—just look at me. See my eyes and nose and lips? Remember my face good so that you see it on the inside of the black hood— Oooo I shouldn't say that but it's all so important to me, that when after—when you are dead they'll come to be with me and grieve. But if they don't? I couldn't stand it, I must feel them all around me, they must be a loving family —all around me, they must feel so sorry for me—because I am a mother with no son.

LOOP: Nothin' nothin' nothin' . . .

MRS. LOOP: Whut?

LOOP: I'm gonna be nothin' (*He rubs his feet on the floor.*) nothin'—so? Mother, who's gonna be with you? The folks you like?

MRS. LOOP: Yes. But they've made my life very hard. I need them though. You wouldn't know being a man. You're my son and if you were a minister I couldn't be more proud. I'm saying everything now. I remember when you got tat-tooed. You said it was manly. I wasn't more proud. (*She opens her bag and lifts out a square package.*) I remember when Howard bopped me. Take some fruitcake, son. Your father was jealous of me, you wouldn't dream that I was a good-looking girl to look at me now, but I was and Howard was very jealous of me. You look like me you know, when I was young. And he would say he'd kill me too, you know, even before you were born when you was just the fruit of my womb. I'm an old woman now and have not one bit a thing. When I was young I coulda had a lot, cause of my looks. I didn't want anything, just to be happy.

Loop: Mom—wouldn't it be wonderful if I could make myself invisible? Then I could go away. They couldn't find me. You and me would finally be let alone.

Mrs. Loop: Yes, it would be wonaful (*She's almost in a trance.*) Oscar, I forgive you for wanting me to die.

Loop: Mama, I never meant that really.

Mrs. Loop: I know you didn't. I'm sorry I said that.

Loop: You couldn't die anyway', cause I'd give you the spice insects.

Narrator: They look at each other as if he's a tot learning to walk. Noise is heard, it's time for Loop to die. When he's dead he won't see any more.

Warden: Hello Mrs. Loop and Oscar. Mrs. Loop go to my cousin Hattie, she's outside waiting to take you home with her. Oscar you come with me to the middle of town. Right?

Loop: Right, yes yes, right. I'm bad. But I'm gonna keep my feet together when I swing like a soldier.

Mrs. Loop: He's gonna look like a minister high on the pulpit above the congregation. I'm going to dress respectably.

SCENE EIGHT

Narrator: Majorie in a whorey mood, walking with two drunken blokes in the field.

MAJORIE: Runnin' bastud. Futz's so scared now.

SUGFORD: Aaaa harrrr that's good.

BUFORD: Pooos. Scared yella. Uuuuuuuuuuuch my stomach hurts.

MAJORIE: You have your stomach—Cy's not gonna have his.

SUGFORD: Yeah yeah.

BUFORD: Gal that was a *creazzy* thing to do with you. I wouldn't ha' done that, I'm bagged.

SUGFORD: You bagged? I'm alive.

MAJORIE: I'm alive too.

NARRATOR: She sits on the grass, the two get down on her sides.

MAJORIE: I'm wanting excitement.

SUGFORD: Maybe you need to get banged.

BUFORD: Me too.

MAJORIE: (*Laughing high*) What for?

BUFORD: Wha'ya mean, wha'for? For fun.

NARRATOR: He picks up a stone and throws it at her. She catches it and starts playing with it, hands cupping it like its a baby chick.

MAJORIE: Let's go nuts us three then clean up somehow.

SCENE NINE

NARRATOR: A little time later.

MAJORIE: Noooooot enough noooot enough!

SUGFORD: We gotta fix it good.

BUFORD: Gal, you're a pig. (*He coughs; then laughs like a madman.*)

SUGFORD: Yeah, she's a pig. We should chop her up with the other one.

MAJORIE: It's too late and I'd be dreary eating. I'm revengeful. Look I know where it is! His sow. Let's kill her. Let's kill his pig!

BUFORD: So what for? So? Fat pig wants to kill a pig.

SUGFORD: Wou'nt that be like killing yu sister?

MAJORIE: Both of you are like mice! Just wanting . . .

BUFORD: Git off it.

SUGFORD: Girly git off it. You're just askin' for it.

BUFORD: You don't know how you could end up.

MAJORIE: You don' have to do nothin'. I'll just do it.

SUGFORD: Why?

MAJORIE: Because I want to.

SUGFORD: Buf?

BUFORD: Okay.

SCENE TEN

NARRATOR: Everything is the same.

SUGFORD: Who wants it?

MAJORIE: She's a dirty dirty thing.

SUGFORD: I'm getting away from totty. You don' want to stay here any more, do you?

BUFORD: No. Let's just gooooo.

(BUFORD *and* SUGFORD *run off.*)

MAJORIE: Come back, ya chicken bastards.

NARRATOR: Hell hath no fury like a woman scorned by a man—for a pig.

SCENE ELEVEN

NARRATOR: In the prison cell Futz sits very hard. He's blowing out his cheeks and binding his nostrils close to the bone.

CY: Huh uuh-huh-hh-uuh- Oooooook huuhhhhoooookiiooook huuuuuh -uuuuhuh-huuuuoook ook Amaaaanddddaaaaa I mis you sooooo, my molly Amaaaaandaaaaa I miiiiiiiisssss youuuuuuu. Tain't faih my faymale. You were good to me 'nd I was sooo good to you. You ate corn 'nd sleep beside me. We tried to go to church but they wouldn't let us in so I'd read you the Bible at home. My mother was a good Protistin, she'd love you too. Mother, get back in your grave you're stinkin' up the green world!

(WARDEN *comes in.*)

WARDEN: Behave yourself. Isn't there any decency in you? Dishonorin' your parents memory screaming out blasphemies in prison.

CY: Warden, you look like a bad drawing of God.

WARDEN: Futz, I should let the folks take you to them. I should hand you over to them. They'd teach your dead body manners.

CY: You want a war.

WARDEN: I want you legally killed.

CY: You don't have to fear I'll rape your mother she's too old. Or your daughter she's got your bad teeth. Warden, why don't you kill your wife and kids? You know that you're unhappy.

WARDEN: I'm a normal man, Futz. It's you that's unhappy. And you've caused treachery.

CY: I wasn't near people. They came to me and looked under my trousers all the way up to their dirty hearts. They minded my *own* life. O you're making me be so serious. And I'm only serious with my wife.

WARDEN: Your what?

CY: (*Screaming*) My wife my *wife*! And how many tits does your wife have? Mine has twelve.

WARDEN: You're ranting, animal.

CY: If I was wi' her I'd be grunting.

SCENE TWELVE

NARRATOR: It's Satz's place. Dirty. The old man, son and mother are there.

MOTHER: Majorie's such a bitch.

FATHER: It must ov been the bug's fault when she was born.

MOTHER: What d'ye mean?

FATHER: I saw a bug on your stomach when she yipped.

MOTHER: I was clean when the child was born.

FATHER: Clean as a swamp.

MOTHER: Swamp! Swamp! No. It was pure water that they had on me.

FATHER: Pig piss it was! Why, woman, you're still slying and lying!

MOTHER: I'm not gon' to say the story any more.

FATHER: Look! Look! The girl is not mine. Not my dotter.

MOTHER: She is she is she is!

FATHER: She is my dotter? Then why did the bugs sit on your knees crying prayers to heaven?

MOTHER: It didna happen!

FATHER: It could ov been you with the pig and him—like it was her!

MOTHER: I'll call my son. (*Screaming*) Ned! Ned!

(BROTHER NED *comes in.*)

FATHER: Ned Ned—be dead!

MOTHER: Hear him!

FATHER: Everythin's made her nervous, Ned. She's mad again.

BROTHER NED: Don't be mad. Majorie'll get her honor back again I'm going to kill Futz.

FATHER: Don't do it alone, take someone with you.

BROTHER NED: I want to myself.

MOTHER: (*Crying*) But wash with pure water, don' leave the blood.

FATHER: He could leave the blood. There's no disgrace in fightin' for his sister.

BROTHER NED: HAHuuuhahahashus hahhas hohaaahh-Mother, don't fret I won' leave the blood.

MOTHER: Before you go, will you have somethin' to eat?

SCENE THIRTEEN

NARRATOR: He's in the prison with Cy. Ned.

CY: Boy boy boy. You want to kill me. Why?

BROTHER NED: My family.

CY: I've got none just a sow.

BROTHER NED: You make my brains red.

CY: I'll tell you peace.

BROTHER NED: (*Screaming*) Shut up shut up! I don't want to know you!

CY: You don't have to know me—just let me be.

BROTHER NED: (*Cold fury*) Your neck should be boiled.

CY: That's what I don't want to happen to my sow.

BROTHER NED: She'll die too.

CY: Now why Ned why do you want to kill the animal?

BROTHER NED: (*Seething*) You make my brains red!

(*He stabs* CY.)

NARRATOR: (*Ironical*) Amanda—there's someone here he needs you. Yes.

Blackout

Who Do You Want,
Peire Vidal?

WHO DO YOU WANT, PEIRE VIDAL? ran at the Theatre for the New City from April 29 to May 23, 1982, starring Valerie Charles and Ron Nakahara. Ernest Abuba Directed, Kuni Mikami Composed the music, Chaim Gitter designed the Lighting, Mike Sullivan the Set, and Nikki Carlino was the Production Stage Manager.

Characters

TOM OGGI   A Japanese-American university professor
RENATA BURG   A German terrorist (German accent)
JOSEPH   An actor
JOSEPHINE   An actress
PEIRE VIDAL   A Provençal troubadour poet (French accent)
LOMBARDA   A Provençal troubadour poet (French accent)
BERNAT   Lombarda's Lover (French accent)

Setting

Bare stage. Minimum of props. A life-sized evil-looking dummy of a security guard is in view.

Two actors play several roles in different situations that are interrelated and sometimes unrelated. Visual and verbal patterns are interwoven; word, sound, and image reinforce and elucidate each other. All positive, comic, and dark values should be explored.

OGGI: (*Tense, passionate, repressed*) I am about to enter beautiful France. When one stops to consider the importance of the act of an entrance—few acts can produce such extremes of emotion—the utmost bliss of a vacation in France. My own country is America. I am a university professor with a passionate interest and love for France. In my opinion France is the most highly developed country in Europe. I have a cousin who is a clerk in an expensive hotel in Nice. A hotel with a stereo in every room. Not a bad job for a boy who sells his body to Japanese-American college professors. Of course this is a disconnected monologue! Whatever does one do when one is being inspected for contraband or tiny weapons of destruction. Don't we make a good match? The security guard and I. (OGGI *snaps a picture.*) I'm O.K., you're O.K., baby! (OGGI *bows.*)

RENATA: (*Angry*) Fascist! Fascist! Bourgeois capitalist pig! Stop searching my body! He's touching my body intimately. Of course I love you, angel. But you've got to be self-critical! We are confronted by two types of social contradictions! Those between ourselves and the enemy! I ought to develop that thought for the article I want to write: In the Conditions Prevailing in Europe Today. In France particularly the contradictions among the people compromise the contradictions within the working class, the contradictions within the peasantry. Shit! Mao said it better! I wonder if this guard has ever read Mao! He looks like he rides a motorcycle! An ugly French rat! A dirty little materialistic French rat! Vulgar! Vulgar! Past the Pyrenees you're not really white! Aaaalalalalala! (*To audience*) Latins are lazy! Racist too! How the French oppress those North Africans! The French are so arrogant! Arrogant and absurd! (*She spits at the Guard and exits.*)

JOSEPH: (*Enters, angry*) I'm going to be a Japanese-American tourist with a camera! And you're going to be a German terrorist with dynamite!

JOSEPHINE: I thought it was a bomb! Thank you!

JOSEPH: Oh. Sorry. A bomb! Satisfied? These characters are just stock figures anyway. There's no socially relevant point of view in this piece. It's just bits and pieces—bits and pieces!

JOSEPHINE: It's a very good vehicle! It can be a tour de force! To play one character after another and another! Then another!

JOSEPH: That's your opinion! Anyway, I'm having domestic troubles. My wife is on a dig in Mexico and I think she's in love with the head of the archeological expedition.

JOSEPHINE: You're just depressed, that's all. Why have a wife who doesn't love you or your noble craft? Listen, I want to do this play but I need you to do it with me.

JOSEPH: You're too difficult! You're not consistent. You know that we were supposed to rehearse that skit I wrote for television!

JOSEPHINE: Television! Impossible! It's not suitable for television. Not in France!

JOSEPH: It's for Swedish television! Now can we rehearse it?

JOSEPHINE: Not right now! We're working on something else right now.

JOSEPH: (*Pedantic*) Everything connects in the universe! Theatre is dynamic. An exploration of illusion, changing circumstances. That's from an article I wrote recently for a theatre journal in America. (*Angry*) We really do understand each other. We get along very well!

BLACKOUT

(*Morse code sounds.* VOICE *is heard saying:*)

SUSPEND THE BLACKNESS
NEWS IS MY VIEW OF SEEING, QUESTIONS,
    SPACES.

(*Lights*)

JOSEPH: The skit works! Isn't it great! What do you think?

JOSEPHINE: (*Mimicking*) Isn't it great! What do you think? It's got nothing to do with Tom Oggi, the Japanese-American university professor, or Renata Burg, the terrorist!

JOSEPH: So what?! It doesn't matter.

JOSEPHINE: Arbitrary! Ar-bit-rar-y! Will you help me look for a new apartment? I must move to a larger place. My nephew is coming to stay with me. Why are we here? I forget what we're here for . . . this place . . . what's our purpose?

JOSEPH: Ha! Existential! You're goin' existential on me, baby!

JOSEPHINE: (*To the audience*) I need a larger apartment.

JOSEPH: I'll help you look, I'll help you look, really, really I will. But now—the play!

JOSEPHINE: I don't like this play. The roles are not interesting.

JOSEPH: What do you want? Provençal troubadours? Peire Vidal!

PEIRE VIDAL: I came from Toulouse. My father was a furrier. I sing better than any man in the world. (*Acappella*)

> Long I searched for
> What I always need
> The greatest victories
> In love and deed.

I am one of the maddest fellows who ever lived. I believe in truth—truth is whatever I want or whatever happens to please me. I will always succeed in making my songs lighter than anyone else's.

JOSEPHINE: Why should you play Peire Vidal? I want to play him!

PEIRE VIDAL: Nothing can quell the fire in Peire Vidal!

JOSEPH: I give this role originality and feeling. And technically I'm a superior and more interesting actor than you, Josephine. Now let me continue the part of Peire Vidal. A song.

PEIRE VIDAL: (*A cappella*)

> I fell in love at night
> I always find what I want!

> (*Blackout*)

(*Lights*)

OGGI: During World War II thousands of Japanese-Americans were deprived of their homes and business. Their lives came to a stop. And they were forced to live in concentration camps. It was a choice that the president of the U.S.A. made. (*Pause*) Though I am vacationing in La Belle France, snapping pictures of the famous historic places during the day and practicing my French conversation in the bars at night . . . I hold in my heart a poison flower of hatred for the cruel and bigoted whites of America who made my parents sicken and grow old before their time—who took from them—my sweet and gentle parents—their home and their land. My grandparents came from Japan and my parents were born in America. They were prosperous flower growers in California. When I was a little tot I would play in the greenhouse my grandfather kept. I remember an incident that happened when I was three. It was a day when I had one of my temper tantrums. I had become frustrated because I could not catch a butterfly. . . . I was in the greenhouse running and jumping all over the flowers, I was pushing the pots of plants over and rolling them and watching them smash against the stone wall. My grandfather stood by in a corner of the garden with my mother beside him. She was holding my little white cap. She wanted to catch me and restrain my violence but my grandfather would not permit her to go to me. He stood there in silence and allowed me to ruin his flowers. He said that I would grow up to be an artist. I did not become an artist. Instead I became a professor in an American university. One is granted long vacations during summertime and there are other intervals with time away from the university. That's why I can spend a long time in France. . . . In France I put away all my anxiety, my fear, fear that makes my palms cold and wet and gives me stomach ulcers. In France, I pretend to be an aristocrat or a world-famous scholar. But I never completed my doctoral project. I never finished writing a scholarly book—I who have given important ideas to other scholars, many of them younger than myself ... those white bastards who write and publish constantly! Stupid and arrogant men! They write the books that I was meant to write! They live in beautiful large homes and are waited on by young Greek male servants—and they touch the nylon-covered crotches of their female students! I was the one who was supposed to be an important scholar of Medieval European literature. Who turned the wheel of fortune against me? It was myself! But nobody is to pity me! Il vaut mieux faire envie que pitie!

JOSEPH: (*Testy*) I didn't know the Americans put Japanese-American citizens into concentration camps. Did they put any German-Americans in the camps with them?

JOSEPHINE: No German- or Italian-Americans were interned during World War II. Only Japs!

JOSEPH: (*Angry*) Japanese! (*Pause*) And those are the facts?

JOSEPHINE: Yes. Those are the facts of American history. Racism! It was a racist policy to imprison Japanese-Americans. Do you like the character Tom Oggi?

JOSEPH: Yes. I want to play him. But I can't rehearse this evening. My wife is coming back from the archeological expedition. (*Pointing to the Security Guard*). Why doesn't he say something!? There are flaws in this formless play. It doesn't make any sense! I want to ask you a question. Do you think that my wife will ever complete her doctoral project and get a high-paying university position?

JOSEPHINE: How should I know!

JOSEPH: I don't think she'll ever finish her doctoral project. And she'll never get a job in a university except perhaps as a file clerk. (*Pause*) Who's directing this play?

JOSEPHINE: We both are. (*Melodramatically*) The play is also moving along by itself like life! A moment ago you

mentioned the Security Guard—you know I think he's a
very interesting character—he stands for oppressive
force. Never! Never! Never!

JOSEPH: Never? What do you mean?

JOSEPHINE: You are right. Your wife will never get a job in
a university except perhaps as a file clerk!

RENATA: Before I became a revolutionary I was a nurse in
a hospital in Vietnam. I took care of handicapped orphans, children of American soldiers and the Vietnamese
women who had abandoned them. Many of the fathers
were black! My work was routine and tiring but the impact of sustained intimate contact with the little orphans
had a profound effect. I became a pacifist. A young French
engineer I had met asked me to marry him. We became
engaged and spent a lot of time going to the cinema and at-
tending left-wing political seminars. On our days off we
would load up his convertible with the orphans for rides
into the country. I suppose we were happy. He'd call me
and I would—(*Telephone rings,* RENATA *answers.*) William
darling, you have a day off today—no more tasks to
do—But you don't want to take the orphans for a ride in
the country—you are irritable? Have you tried to deter-
mine why you are so anxious? A death anxiety? Diffuse
anxiety? Mutilation anxiety? Shame anxiety also? Darling, the theme of existence is anxiety. Yes, of course.
(*Laughs*) No, I'm not laughing at your anxieties. They are
not minor anxieties, they are major ones. Yes, darling. No,
I don't think you're inadequate or hostile. Darling, I don't
know why you fear that we will have a car accident. You
know darling, two or three days preceding a menstrual cy-
cle many women fell anxious. The most universal discom-
forts are bloatedness, irritability, and depression. I didn't
say that you are turning into a woman! You're saying
crazy things now! Why! Why! No! No! Yes, I agree with
you—we are making constant demands on each other's
time! No, I have not made a name for myself in the world
yet—how could I with you taking up my days and nights!
You put pressure on me! And I can't do my serious work!

You're acting crazy! Why are you belching into the phone at me? No, you will not take away my precious time anymore, William. And I'm not interested in home, children, and traditional female roles. (RENATA *hangs up the telephone.*) Well, that relationship is finished. (*Pause.*) There is one final alternative to the problem of realizing my potential strength—more self-knowledge and significant social action!

JOSEPHINE: Renata's lover became intensely jealous and that's why the relationship had to end. William, the lover of Renata, is intellectually inferior.

JOSEPH: Who is Renata?

JOSEPHINE: Renata is the woman terrorist! This play is an excellent vehicle to demonstrate an actor's skill! To become one character and then another and another and another. However, I'm disturbed about the ideology of the play. I don't see any emerging feminist sensibility. It's a maze of pointless wanderings. (*Pause*) I have an idea! Renata, the anarchist, meets a woman troubadour! Surprised? the word troubadour makes you think of a medieval gallant singing love songs to his lady fair—but there were some troubadours who were women. Their existence and the songs they wrote raise new questions about the role of women in medieval culture. Yes. Renata meets Lombarda, a woman troubadour from Toulouse—

JOSEPH: Where do they meet?

JOSEPHINE: In a little inn.

RENATA: I broke off the relationship with William because it was ridiculous and self-destructive. (*Pause*) What kind of poetry do you write?

LOMBARDA: Some of my poetry is elegant, some is blunt.

RENATA: Do you ever write proud poetry? Poetry that has as its theme pride and courage?

LOMBARDA: Yes, I've written poems about pride. I've written poems about happiness and about being hurt in love.

LOMBARDA: Beautiful knight
You're the one today
That I yearn for
Yesterday I worshipped
Your lustful sister. (*Laughs*)

One of my lovers was a man who had no toes on his right foot. I noticed it after a whole month of sleeping with him. Whenever we fought he would thrust his wretched foot at me—he wanted to gain my sympathy. One night I told him that I no longer wanted to see him and that I no longer had pity for him. He began raving—

BERNAT: I am Bernat and I love you, Lombarda! If you forsake me I'll throw you down in the street. I'll shove my fist through the windows of churches!

LOMBARDA: Frankly, I don't give a damn, Bernat! I'm tired of being a pawn in a man's strategic interests, my father's or my clan's. Like all women I have no legal status of my own. But I still have the power to choose the thing that is most important to me—my poetry!

BERNAT: No one is more dangerous than a woman who wants self-realization. That kind of woman is worse than the bubonic plague. I will fix it so that you will never leave me, Lombarda!

LOMBARDA: (*To* RENATA) He took long iron nails and he nailed my feet to the floor. He could not bear to see how far I could go—with anxiousness and dedication—to walk on the razor's edge with fear and ecstasy.

RENATA: We can look into each other's eyes and exchange terror for terror, pleasure for pleasure.

(*BLACKOUT*)

(*MIDNIGHT SPECIAL: CON ED FAILS BLACKOUT LATE SHOW*)

(*Lights*)

JOSEPH: Is this a comedy-tragedy? We need an action scene. A sword fight! A duel! A duel between Peire Vidal and Lombarda!

(They begin to duel, and it gradually turns into a dance.)

PEIRE VIDAL: I never met a woman troubadour but I'd rather see than be one. *(Laughs)*

LOMBARDA: We are a neglected group of poets.

PEIRE VIDAL: I'd like to hear some of your poetry, Lombarda.

LOMBARDA: Sweet friend, I'm telling the truth
                That I've never been without desire.

PEIRE VIDAL: Is that the end? Isn't there any more?

LOMBARDA: Yes, there is more. But I want you to contemplate those two simple lines. Repeat them.

PEIRE VIDAL: Sweet friend, I'm telling the truth
                That I've never been without desire.

O, Lombarda! You are a very mysterious woman.

LOMBARDA: Peire, you are a very mysterious man. I have heard that at night you wear a wolf skin. And that you do wild things.

PEIRE VIDAL: A poet is a man. Men can do wild things.

LOMBARDA: And women too!

PEIRE VIDAL: I am the maddest poet that ever lived. I'm good in many things.

LOMBARDA: Of course you are. And what a thrilling idea! Come for me at 7:00 and—and—and—

PEIRE VIDAL: And wear my wolf skin.

JOSEPH: Peire Vidal and Lombarda are going to be lovers? Is that what will happen?

JOSEPHINE: *(Melodramatic)* They are romantic. The world becomes their private bedchamber where they can glimpse the cosmos. But something disrupts this narcissistic viewpoint. Their dream.

JOSEPH: What?

JOSEPHINE: Lombarda is aware of society's injustice towards women. Listen to the dialogue between Peire Vidal and Lombarda the woman troubadour.

PEIRE VIDAL: What a clear starless night. My Lombarda, my Lombarda, my Lombarda!

LOMBARDA: Peire, tonight is a night for poets. I remember the first poem that I ever wrote. I was twelve years old.

PEIRE VIDAL: Your hair was long.

LOMBARDA: No, it was short.

PEIRE VIDAL: O.

LOMBARDA: I was called the ice princess. If we understand our nature we can understand the universe. (LOMBARDA *leans against* PEIRE VIDAL *and he jabs his elbow into her side.*) O, that hurts. Why do you jab your elbow into my ribs like a cruel sword. I leaned against you like a sweet friend and your arm is unfriendly against me.

PEIRE VIDAL: You confuse my intellect. And you perplex me. I feel that you are my enemy.

LOMBARDA: Peire, trust me!

PEIRE VIDAL: I don't want to trust you.

LOMBARDA: I'm a poet like you, Peire Vidal!

PEIRE VIDAL: Yes, it's true that you are a poet. But I want a woman not a poet! There is a certain kind of woman that I long for.

LOMBARDA: Am I not her?

PEIRE VIDAL: You are not her. You are not her. You are not her.

(*BLACKOUT*)

(*Morse code static*)

(*Lights*)

JOSEPH: This is the fifth night of rehearsal and the play is still bits and pieces. There is no logical direction.

JOSEPHINE: Why did you interrupt the scene between Peire Vidal and Lombarda?

JOSEPH: It's you who interrupt the scene!

JOSEPHINE: Are you worried about your wife leaving you? Leaving you for the archeological guide! You're a worried wreck! You're torn torn torn up with worry! (*Pause*) And what does that thing represent—the security guard! Is he a symbol of watching!? Observing!? It's as if we're blindfolded in this play.

JOSEPH: Relax! We are finding our way. At the moment we are both walking through the play. It's an excellent vehicle to demonstrate an actor's skill.

JOSEPHINE: Phony aesthetics! (*Mimicking*) It's an excellent vehicle blah blah blah . . . Explain to me why I want to bump my head against the wall—why the play doesn't move except randomly. Why I want to put on clown make-up!

(*BLACKOUT. Morse Code.* VOICE:)

I LIKE YOU TO TOUCH ME WHILE WATCHING CABLE T.V. WHAT'S SO BAD ABOUT THAT REQUEST?

(*Lights*)

JOSEPH: You're having a temper tantrum. When you're calm we'll run through my television skit. This time I'll play the French gigolo!

(*BLACKOUT. Morse Code.*)

(*Lights*)

JOSEPHINE: The dialogue in that skit sounds like real conversation.

JOSEPH: But just when an interesting confrontation is about to take place—the lights go out!

(*BLACKOUT. Morse Code.*)

(*Lights*)

OGGI: When I look back now to my youth I realize that I have always loved French culture. During my long adolescence I desired very much to own a pair of 18th century French porcelain busts that I saw in an antique store. It was a marquis and his lady. I pretended that they were my father and mother. In my imagination I would stroke the heads and put my hot cheek against the creamy white faces of the sculptures. I understood in the deepest part of my being that they were symbols of La Belle France and that France was for me a heavenly ladder of artistic and cultural refinement. At night I would whirl around the parlor in our home wearing a grey and pink-flowered silk brocaded cape that my mother wore to music recitals. I would pretend that I was the young blond son of the marquis and his lady. The back of my legs would begin to tingle as I twirled around and around the piano. Often I would feel the compulsion to thrust my body into the edges of the piano stool. My mother would worry as she watched me torture myself when I madly tried to lengthen and narrow my own round nose into what I believed was the proper nose shape of my fantasy; the little son of the Marquis and his lady. The more pain that I submitted my body to the more I believed I would be able to change myself into my French dream child. When I was nine years old I was given art lessons. There was a teacher that I was especially fond of, a Dutch nun with a long face and a wall-eye. I always had a pleasant feeling as I watched her, her eye fixed at its unique angle. The children had cruel names for her, "twist-eye" and "curse-eye." She was a traditionalist in her method of instructing children and commanded us to copy exactly the paintings of the 19th century masters. She hated any originality and often hit the children's knuckles if they dared to attempt any new ideas. I never felt it in my heart to disobey her wishes. I copied the paintings as she requested us to do. She had an unusual habit of placing yellow notepaper folded to a sharp point between her upper arms. The children would laugh at her antics and I would feel a lump of anger in my throat when they mocked her. It was during World War II and my favorite fantasy was that the children were all sent to the gas chambers in Poland. All the laughers who ridiculed my precious nun. One day before Easter vacation she asked all of us to pray for Generalissimo Franco who was ill and dying. I felt very sad as the nun explained to us the goodness and extreme benevolence of the Generalissimo to orphans and the poor. My hands grew cold when I saw that her own hands were trembling as she told of the betrayal of Franco by the U.S.A. That night I dreamed that I won a lot of money on a radio quiz show and that the Dutch nun and I went to France and Spain and visited the great museums. In my dream the nun turned into my beloved grandfather who had said that I would become an artist. During those evil times when my parents, all my relatives, and I were incarcerated in an American concentration camp, she was the only non-Japanese person that I felt affection for— that I didn't want to kill. I wanted to kill all the white people—assassinate the president. I wanted most of all to kill the children!

JOSEPH: I can't go on. My brain's out of control. This character, Oggi, upsets me! He upsets me!

JOSEPHINE: Your domestic problems again! Is that what's on your mind?

JOSEPH: My mind starts churning! Everything becomes unbearable! What difference does it make if I'm an actor or a murderer!

JOSEPHINE: Stop being so melodramatic!

JOSEPH: You bitch!

JOSEPHINE: Shut your mouth!

JOSEPH: Don't call me melodramatic again! I want them, the audience, to know that when I decide to act in a particular play—it's because I'm ready to walk in a lake of blood!

JOSEPHINE: Artaud! I'm going to vomit! Horseshit!

JOSEPH: There are two intensely frustrated and disillusioned characters in this play—!

JOSEPHINE: When is rehearsal over?

JOSEPH: Do you know that my wife might divorce me?

JOSEPHINE: I don't care! We are rehearsing now! Be attentive to the present!

(*BLACKOUT*)

JOSEPHINE: That blackout was not necessary!

JOSEPH: In my opinion it was. Thank you, madam!

RENATA: Calm. I was calm when I made my decision to become a member of a large powerful international movement actively engaged in overthrowing reactionary governments. I was assigned to partake in political kidnappings. I was ecstatic as I planned my offensive against oppressive forces. What I was before my political conversion I would never be again! It happened one night in Paris, a cold night in November. I was in a cafe and struck up a conversation with a man I had never met before, a Japanese-American tourist. I told him about my experience in Vietnam. He had a very intense expression and smoked continuously. His eyes were fixed at the center of my face, I think he was staring at my lips or my nose—yes, he seemed to be looking at my nose a great deal. It's possible to look at someone directly in the face but really to be looking at the nose solely. He tapped his knee with his forefinger as if he were keeping time to music. I didn't think that he was attracted to me sexually. Whenever he spoke I noticed that he didn't finish his sentences but nodded at me as though he were encouraging me to finish the sentence for him.

OGGI: So, you had a painful experience in Vietnam.

RENATA: To be a nurse in a hospital was not sufficient for my life. (*Pause*) Can you understand?

OGGI: I understand very well. There is something more that we must do. In my case, I must write and publish books. Someday, someday—

RENATA: But that's not all that you want to do. There is something more—

OGGI: Something more than mouldering away in an American university—

RENATA: You want to do something really worthwhile with your life—

OGGI: I must do it! I was scarred and emotionally battered—

RENATA: During the period of confinement that your family and you suffered during the war. You were in a concentration camp in the U.S.A. And that time—

OGGI: And that time is a missing piece of the puzzle, the puzzle of my life. I brood all the time—

RENATA: I brood also.

OGGI: When I force myself to remember that terrible time —I am not able to understand—

RENATA: Why you have not taken revenge. (*Pause*) You and I are fragile survivors.

OGGI: I had a friend once . . . a long time ago. He was a scholar like myself. A medievalist. He was Greek-American. Anyway, I gave him a lot of ideas, important ideas that he incorporated into his first published book. Somehow he had found a way to convince publishers that his manuscripts were worthy of publication—(*Bitterly*) unlike my own of course.

RENATA: He was not a fragile survivor.

OGGI: I never wanted to renounce my honor or integrity—to flatter those who had power—those who could have helped me in my career. I believe that my old friend did—

RENATA: That he flattered those who could help him professionally. Tom, that is not unusual.

OGGI: The only time that I remember him being vulnerable was when he and his wife were separated—

RENATA: Then he needed your friendship, your strength, and your calm.

OGGI: I am not so calm.

RENATA: I know.

OGGI: But I am a sympathetic man—

RENATA: You have a tender heart.

OGGI: Do you know why I love French culture? Why I am a Francophile?

RENATA: I think that you have a lot of reasons.

OGGI: Because the French are an infinitely wise and cultivated race. They have a saying: On prend la vie du bon coté.

RENATA: One takes the good aspects of life. And so you have some cheer in your soul also.

OGGI: Sometimes I am quite depressed—

RENATA: And cruel. Probably you were a sickly child who needed a great deal of devotion—

OGGI: Why do you think that I am cruel, Renata?

RENATA: Because you are a disappointed man.

OGGI: I have been very disappointed by those who I thought were my friends. When Nicholas, my friend, separated from his wife—

RENATA: You lived together a short while.

OGGI: Yes. During the cool summer evenings we would take walks along the bridge—

RENATA: And you would return to the apartment yawning and satisfied to have spent time together.

OGGI: Yes. There was a satisfaction in being together.

RENATA: But he betrayed you.

OGGI: What?

RENATA: You heard me. He betrayed you.

OGGI: He and his wife had a reconciliation. The next time we met it was by sheer accident—in a photocopy store—

Renata: He was having copies of a manuscript reproduced to send off to a publisher. You hated him then.

Oggi: I'm an intense man. Sometimes when I glance at myself in the mirror—I see someone—

Renata: Someone in hell.

Oggi: That's a damned thing to say! (*Bitterly*) You have no right.

Renata: Forgive me, I didn't mean it that way—exactly. What I meant was that you have never cried—you have never allowed yourself to cry—

Oggi: Wrong. You are so wrong. I cried when my beloved grandfather died. (*Pause*) I think that you must have a pair of beautiful breasts. You ought to enjoy—

Renata: Being a woman. (*Pause*) Tom, we are both so alienated from this monstrous society.

Oggi: Really, you ought to enjoy being a woman. Just lie back and let me fuck you in my imagination.

Renata: I've said something to hurt you.

Oggi: Fuck you! You long-nosed bitch!

Renata: You are trying to get me angry at you.

Oggi: When I was a little tyke I thought that the nozzle of the enema bag was a magic wand!

Renata: Tom, I thought that perhaps you were a man I could really talk to.

Oggi: You have a long aristocratic nose.

Renata: You are full of hate.

Oggi: Marie, Marie, I have no time for you.

Renata: Renata, my name is Renata.

Oggi: Marie . . . I think a French woman is often named Marie.

Renata: I'm not French.

OGGI: If only I had met you ten years ago, Marie. I would have asked you to—O, my God! Marie, have you ever seized the reins of a stallion and sped across the hills, leaving the stars and the trees behind your shadow!

RENATA: Tom, you're a romantic fellow.

OGGI: A long time ago . . . I wanted to be an artist. Do you think I'm lying?

RENATA: No. I wanted to be a neurosurgeon when I was fifteen. I became a nurse instead. (*Pause*) I have never gone to bed with a man like you.

OGGI: (*Moves away quickly.*) You mean, a university professor?

JOSEPH: Does this scene take place in broad daylight?

JOSEPHINE: (*Angry*) Don't stop the scene between Oggi and Renata Burg!

JOSEPH: What happens to the other characters!? Peire Vidal! Lombarda! Bernat! And I don't understand the significance of the Security Guard!

JOSEPHINE: He's always there! Right there! (*She points to the figure.*) The play is focusing on Renata Burg and Tom Oggi!

JOSEPH: What are they going to do?! What is the play leading up to?!

JOSEPHINE: An event—that's all! Are you trying to alienate me?! (*Reflective*) Maybe the audience should be closer.

JOSEPH: (*Angry*) I'm on the verge of quitting!

JOSEPHINE: If the audience were closer . . .

JOSEPH: Quitting the show!

JOSEPHINE: (*To audience*) If the audience were closer they would be part of the event.

JOSEPH: (*Trying to get her attention.*) There was another sex change of a man into a woman reported in the papers yesterday!

JOSEPHINE: Please! Give your attention to the present and not to yesterday's news about transsexuals! Thank you, sir! I'm trying to work out something new!

JOSEPH: Either a socially relevant point of view is demonstrated in the play—or else I'm quitting! At least let's have the Japanese—American university professor and the German terrorist commit a skyjacking! That might interest a producer! (*Ironic*) Do you intend to have a climax? A resolution of some kind?

JOSEPHINE: Not in the conventional sense.

JOSEPH: (*Walking off, angry.*) I quit!

JOSEPHINE: (*Grabs him and throws him against the wall.*) No!

OGGI: (*Dreamy tone*) It feels good to be flung that way.

JOSEPHINE: I want to arrive at the true shape of this play!

OGGI: After making love I tend to free-associate. Let different images and words fill my consciousness. It calms me.

RENATA: Only the madman is really calm. Antonin Artaud said that.

OGGI: Renata, do you think that you are mad?

RENATA: I think so. I try to escape from myself.

OGGI: None of us are in the habit of being! Simply being!

RENATA: You mean self-aware?

OGGI: What?

RENATA: You heard me. Why do you pretend not to hear?

OGGI: I am play-acting with you, Renata. There are certain key words which either you or I say and they ought to be repeated.

RENATA: Oh. I don't believe that I am self-aware. I ask myself—

OGGI: What have I done with my life.

RENATA: Yes.

OGGI: I have an expensive coffee-table book filled with the masterpieces of French art—

RENATA: I don't care about your coffee-table book filled with the masterpieces of French art. Don't change the subject. You were about to reveal yourself to me.

OGGI: I'm planning a skyjacking.

RENATA: You are cynical. (OGGI *begins to groan horribly.*) What's the matter with you?

OGGI: (*He rubs his chest and abdomen.*) Nothing.

RENATA: Why are you rubbing yourself like that?

OGGI: My bruises. My bruises. I've hurt myself.

RENATA: Let me look at them. I have the right. I'm a nurse. (*She removes his shirt.*) You have some bruises. How did you get them?

OGGI: I was invited to a private home with a swimming pool and I fell several times—

RENATA: Into the swimming pool? (*Pause*) Was there any water in it?

OGGI: It doesn't matter.

RENATA: Your bruises are like a poem.

OGGI: (*Bitterly*) A poem, Renata? Stop it. My room is not even air-conditioned.

RENATA: What has that to do with your lovely bruises?

OGGI: What has that to do with my lovely bruises? Are you a pervert?

RENATA: No. I like the way the sentence sounds. Like a poem.

OGGI: Not in my judgment. Not at all. I don't like it.

RENATA: I have a tape recording of my voice. I don't like it.

OGGI: Renata, why don't you tell the truth about yourself? You can never achieve real intimacy with a man. But you take pleasure in wasting my time in stupid talk.

RENATA: I don't care what you say. I don't care what you say.

OGGI: We could discuss your memories of early childhood, your feelings about sex, the death of close family members, etc. We could discuss your pain.

RENATA: I don't want to talk about things that are no longer important to me. (*Pause*) We'll find a new subject to talk about.

OGGI: (*Speaks like Marlon Brando.*) You little idiot! You don't know yet why you are so attracted to me! I'm going to finally tell you because you're so unbelievably naive! Have you read about the scandal of the International Film Festival and the suppression by the U.S. Customs of Bashiro's *Below The Head*?

RENATA: Of course.

OGGI: It's me! I'm the actor who played the role in the film with the explicit sexual passages. Remember the gory climax?

RENATA: The strangulation and emasculation?

OGGI: It was me.

RENATA: You mean you are the actor in Bashiro's *Below The Head*? You?

OGGI: Me.

RENATA: You are the actor in that sadomasochistic film? I have very mixed emotions about that film and Bashiro in general. He's interested more in ritual than in narrative.

OGGI: Yes, that's true. And all of his themes are typically French. For instance, a love affair between a gangster and a prostitute!

RENATA: I don't think that theme is typically French. A love affair between a gangster and a prostitute.

OGGI: Typically French!

RENATA: Bashiro's film is typically French? But Bashiro is Japanese.

OGGI: (*Speaks like Marlon Brando.*) Of course. But his films are completely early Renoir! Or like photos of Brassai! (*Pause*) Renata, I'd like to share something with you, a secret. Romantic and mysterious adventures have happened to me exactly as if they were scenes from a French film.

JOSEPH: (*He begins to strangle her.*) It's easy to be nice to you. (*He lets her drop to the floor.*) But there are limits. You're a very good-looking woman. You ought to be in movies.

JOSEPHINE: (*Coughing*) Thank you, sir.

JOSEPH: (*He walks away.*) Good-night.

JOSEPHINE: (*Furious. Picks up a gun.*) What about the Security Guard! Renata Burg! Tom Oggi!

JOSEPH: Stop it! We are finished!

JOSEPHINE: Come back! (*She shoots him. As he falls and stumbles with jerking motions all over the area, he instructs her to shoot him again.*)

JOSEPH: (*After each shot.*) Shoot me again! Shoot me again!

(*The shots should cause him to fling around as much as the situation demands—a semiparody of dying with intense body tremors. A pause, and then he says:*)

JOSEPH: That scene doesn't work.

RENATA: I thought it was fine. (*She slowly aims the gun at him.*)

JOSEPH: (*Apprehensively*) Where's Josephine?

(*The lights fade.*)

The End.

By Rochelle Owens

Poetry

Not Be Essence That Cannot Be (1961)
Four Young Lady Poets (1962)
Salt & Core (1968)
I Am the Babe of Joseph Stalin's Daughter (1972)
Poems from Joe's Garage (1973)
The Joe 82 Creation Poems (1974)
The Joe Chronicles, Part 2 (1979)
Shemuel (1979)
French Light (1984)
Constructs (1985)
W.C. Fields in French Light (1986)

Plays

Futz and *What Came After* (1968)
The Karl Marx Play & Others (1974)
The Widow and the Colonel (1977)
Chucky's Hunch (1982); Wordplays 2

Editor

Spontaneous Combustion: Eight New American Plays
   (1972)

Recordings

From a Shaman's Notebook (1968)
The Karl Marx Play (Songs) Galt MacDermot (Music)
   (1974)
Totally Corrupt (1976)
Black Box 17 (1979)

Film

Futz (1969)

Video

Oklahoma Too (1986)

NATIVE SPEECH

BY ERIC OVERMYER

A riveting play, rich in texture and rife with allusion, which provides a chilling vision of civilization about to go belly up. Originally produced at the **Los Angeles Theater Center** in the summer of 1983. Seven males, three females, though one more of each can be used. Single interior set plus an exterior playing area.

BATTERY

BY DANIEL THERRIAULT

Electricity is the central metaphor and expressive image in this unusual love story which takes place in an electrical repair and systems design shop located in Chicago. Therriault has an exceptional ear for American speech patterns, and has been **compared to Sam Shepard and David Mamet for his superb use of language.** First produced in New York at St. Clement's Theater in the Spring of 1981. Two males, one female; single interior set.

Medusa aimed her poisoned
arrow right at Lillian...

Lillian always loved stories about
myths and monsters—until she
found herself inside one, searching
for her lost sister.

Joined by her best friends, Katy
and Maisy, Lillian must cross a sea
guarded by krakens and sirens, race
through a dark forest haunted by
elves and chimeras, and pass through
mountains ruled by griffins and rocs.

Where in this world is Lillian's
sister? Who is the mysterious boy
with the stone medallion? Why
do the monsters hold an ancient
grudge against humanity? And
what is the secret hiding at the
heart of it all?

The
World
of
LANODEKA

This book is a work of fiction. The characters, incidents and dialogue are drawn from the author's imagination and are not to be construed as real. Any resemblance to actual events or persons, living or dead, is entirely coincidental.

THE MONSTER REALM. Copyright © 2014 by Nara Duffie.

Cover art, Lanodeka map and chapter illustrations by Elisabeth Alba. http://www.albaillustration.com

Author photo by Michael Negrete. http://michaelnegrete.com

ISBN 978-0-9849346-5-2

To Andrea

Thank you!

THE MONSTER REALM

A NOVEL BY

Nara Duffie

with Illustrations by Elisabeth Alba

roam
&ramble

To Ray Harryhausen

CONTENTS

The
World
of
LANODEKA

MAP BY ELISABETH ALBA

THE MONSTER REALM

Prologue: A Girl Disappears

Spring Town was a small town. It was named Spring Town because it felt like spring all through the year, cool and sunny and green, then in December it turned cold and rainy and felt like winter.

On every street, leafy trees stood in a line. The branches grew into each other like a canopy, until winter came. Then the empty branches looked tangled and creepy, almost like skeletons.

On a March afternoon, Lillian sat in her room reading *Harry Potter and the Prisoner of Azkaban.* She was ten years old and tall for her age, healthy and strong. She had hazel-green eyes and light brown skin, and her wavy red hair fell to her shoulders. Lillian never wore makeup, not even to church or on birthdays.

Lillian loved mythology and monsters, especially Ray Harryhausen movies. She loved how his stop motion animation made the monsters look mythical instead of real. Ray's monsters were scary without being too scary.

Bluebell, Lillian's older sister, walked through the door. "Are you reading that book *again?*" she teased. "You must have read it a million times."

Lillian put down her book. She was reading the most exciting chapter, the most thrilling part of the whole novel. Then Bluebell strutted in, and Lillian was pulled out of the magical story.

If Lillian even peeked into her sister's room, Bluebell would yell at her to get out. If her mom and dad were around, Bluebell would yell at Lillian later. But she never forgot to yell at Lillian, and she never said she was sorry.

Bluebell wore a royal blue swimsuit and carried a big beach bag. She was sixteen, had dark green eyes and short, curly red hair. She never wore her hair up; she never even wore it in a hair band. She used a lot of dark blue eyeshadow and pale pink lipstick. She was impatient with everyone, especially with Lillian.

"I'm going to a beach party and sleepover, Lillian, and you're not invited," Bluebell smirked. "You'll have to stay home, and let me guess, when I'm gone you're going to watch *Clash of the Titans* for the millionth time, the most boring movie in the world. If by some slim chance you decide to watch something else, it'll